GREETINGS FROM
MELBOURNE
FLA.

GREETINGS FROM
MELBOURNE
FLA.

GREETINGS FROM
MELBOURNE
FLA.

GREETINGS FROM
MELBOURNE
FLA.

GREETINGS FROM
MELBOURNE
FLA.

GREETINGS FROM
MELBOURNE
FLA.

GREETINGS FROM
MELBOURNE
FLA.

GREETINGS FROM
MELBOURNE
FLA.

GREETINGS FROM
MELBOURNE
FLA.

GREETINGS FROM
MELBOURNE
FLA.

GREETINGS FROM
MELBOURNE
FLA.

GREETINGS FROM
MELBOURNE
FLA.

GREETINGS FROM
MELBOURNE
FLA.

GREETINGS FROM
MELBOURNE
FLA.

GREETINGS FROM
MELBOURNE
FLA.

GREETINGS FROM
MELBOURNE
FLA.

GREETINGS FROM
MELBOURNE
FLA.

GREETINGS FROM
MELBOURNE
FLA.

GREETINGS FROM
MELBOURNE
FLA.

GREETINGS FROM
MELBOURNE
FLA.

GREETINGS FROM
MELBOURNE
FLA.

GREETINGS FROM
MELBOURNE
FLA.

GREETINGS FROM
MELBOURNE
FLA.

GREETINGS FROM
MELBOURNE
FLA.

GREETINGS FROM
MELBOURNE
FLA.

GREETINGS FROM
MELBOURNE
FLA.

GREETINGS FROM
MELBOURNE
FLA.

GREETINGS FROM
MELBOURNE
FLA.

GREETINGS FROM
MELBOURNE
FLA.

GREETINGS FROM
MELBOURNE
FLA.

GREETINGS FROM
MELBOURNE
FLA.

GREETINGS FROM
MELBOURNE
FLA.

GREETINGS FROM
MELBOURNE
FLA.

GREETINGS FROM
MELBOURNE
FLA.

GREETINGS FROM
MELBOURNE
FLA.

GREETINGS FROM
MELBOURNE
FLA.

GREETINGS FROM
MELBOURNE
FLA.

GREETINGS FROM
MELBOURNE
FLA.

GREETINGS FROM
MELBOURNE
FLA.

GREETINGS FROM
MELBOURNE
FLA.

GREETINGS FROM
MELBOURNE
FLA.

GREETINGS FROM
MELBOURNE
FLA.

GREETINGS FROM
MELBOURNE
FLA.

GREETINGS FROM
MELBOURNE
FLA.

GREETINGS FROM
MELBOURNE
FLA.

GREETINGS FROM
MELBOURNE
FLA.

GREETINGS FROM
MELBOURNE
FLA.

GREETINGS FROM
MELBOURNE
FLA.

GREETINGS FROM
MELBOURNE
FLA.

GREETINGS FROM
MELBOURNE
FLA.

GREETINGS FROM
MELBOURNE
FLA.

GREETINGS FROM
MELBOURNE
FLA.

GREETINGS FROM
MELBOURNE
FLA.

GREETINGS FROM
MELBOURNE
FLA.

GREETINGS FROM
MELBOURNE
FLA.

GREETINGS FROM
MELBOURNE
FLA.

GREETINGS FROM
MELBOURNE
FLA.

GREETINGS FROM
MELBOURNE
FLA.

GREETINGS FROM
MELBOURNE
FLA.

GREETINGS FROM
MELBOURNE
FLA.

GREETINGS FROM
MELBOURNE
FLA.

GREETINGS FROM
MELBOURNE
FLA.

GREETINGS FROM
MELBOURNE
FLA.

GREETINGS FROM
MELBOURNE
FLA.

GREETINGS FROM
MELBOURNE
FLA.

GREETINGS FROM
MELBOURNE
FLA.

GREETINGS FROM
MELBOURNE
FLA.

GREETINGS FROM
MELBOURNE
FLA.

GREETINGS FROM
MELBOURNE
FLA.

GREETINGS FROM
MELBOURNE
FLA.

GREETINGS FROM
MELBOURNE
FLA.

GREETINGS FROM
MELBOURNE
FLA.

GREETINGS FROM
MELBOURNE
FLA.

GREETINGS FROM
MELBOURNE
FLA.

GREETINGS FROM
MELBOURNE
FLA.

Printed in the USA
CPSIA information can be obtained
at www.ICGtesting.com
CBHW031456030824
12613CB00052B/881

9 798385 410224